150 Opportunities

written by

Richard Wilkins

First published May 1997

Published by cantecia
P O Box 454
Northampton
NN3 2YQ

ISBN   0 9528198 1 3

Cover design by Richard Wilkins
Printed by Candor Print, Northampton

Introduction

Things never run smoothly in a good adventure story.
There's lots of interaction between the good guys
and the bad guys.
There's romance. Hearts get broken.
People get hurt, even die.
Not to mention the twist,
the bit where it doesn't turn out
how you thought it would,
the unexpected outcome!

Sound a bit like your life?
You see, I've worked it out -
I just can't stop life happening to me.
Now, instead of being continually offended by it -
I've joined forces with life.
So, instead of my life being a series of traumas,
it's become one big adventure
in which anything can happen.

My new friend life and I
have written this book together.
We hope you get as much from reading it,
as we did from writing it.

The adventure continues......

DEDICATION

To Gillian, my wife.

Who gives her time that I may write.
Who paves the way that I may talk.

I dedicate this book to your humility, Gillian,
which I cannot reach, but will always love.

The only thing that can ever hurt you
is **your resistance to change.**

Your potential can never be measured
or used up.

Enlightenment isn't switching on the light,
it's seeing in the dark.

Compromise
is more interested in making it work,
than making a point.

Love;
You can stop the flow from you,
but **never** to you...

Fate may provide your journey.
How you travel your journey
is your choice.

Happiness and Unhappiness
are simply the high and low tides
on the edge of a great sea
called contentment.

Constructive criticism
is a well meaning fool.

Pain and pleasure:
Thorns and petals of the same rose.

Good deeds get done,
bad deeds get publicity.

'The now' happens so fast
it cannot be measured,
yet it is the maximum length of time
you will ever have to endure anything.

Excuses are the unlimited disguises of blame.

People, like caterpillars,
think they'll never fly,
and then one day...

Life's a jigsaw.
We can get so wrapped up.
in trying to make the little pieces fit,
that we miss the whole picture.

Kindness has its own language.

Christmas is a stirring of the child within.

You don't know it
if you don't apply it:
'Would you let a surgeon operate on you
who has never held a scalpel
but knows all the theory?'

'You never know what's around the corner'
Wannabet?
Like a fast food drive through,
you'll get what you've ordered.

Change a **can't** to a **could**
and you've got a **chance.**

You don't have to own
to appreciate.

Kindness is investing in a pension fund
that matures after life
and pays out forever.

Each time you act on your imagination
a thought gives birth.
This is creation.

Most people take more care
over choosing a house
than choosing a partner.

It may take a very big shake
to wake you
from a very deep sleep.

Loneliness
is a misunderstanding.
It's simply God
wanting a private word with you.

Birds leap before they fly....

A belief is a preconceived attitude based on the past.

A house is just a building,
a home is anywhere you live.

To listen you need sound.
To hear you need interest.

'There'
isn't where you think.
It's **how** you think.

Observers use others mistakes
as their lessons.

You will find in others
what you look for.

D.I.Y. loving -
it lasts a lifetime!

Security is not having things,
it's not wanting them.

If you applied what you knew,
you'd be amazed at how much you know!

Life **is** a dress rehearsal.

The arrow fired from the bow of truth
causes no lesser wound
than the arrow fired from the bow of hatred.

Ignoring your conscience
allows you to justify anything.

Friendship often survives the relationship
for which it was neglected.

Surrender is having the vision
to see the damage
your pride could cause you.

Jealousy...
the inability to share in anothers joy.

Accepting you've done your best
can free you to go forward
and do better.

Greet criticism
by asking,
'How does that help me?'

Understanding is a warrior
who has never lost a fight
or defeated an opponent.

You will let go in death
what you think you can't in life,
so why wait?

When a dream
joins forces with an intention,
the result is a reality.

A great place to meet,
is on equal terms.

Dark clouds
are sunbeam makers...

People who think these are the bad times
would do well to remember,
the good old times got them here!

People don't die,
they simply go to heaven.
Dying is what happens to people
who still need a body
and believe people in heaven are dead.

Unconditional love
is the flame of a candle,
content to give it's light to anyone.

Legality before morality = brutality.
Morality before brutality = compassion.

A co-incidence
is simply a reply to a cosmic fax
you sent earlier.

Happiness can provide the music,
but sadness can make you listen.

A fear is totally dependent on one thing,
you not wanting it.

A dream can steer you through
a lifetime of realities.

A man who bore a child
would soon lose his appetite for war.

Why lend what you can afford to give?

When you go through
the bottom of one thing
you find yourself
on the top of another.

When someone wins
...other lose.
When someone leads
...others follow.

Sleep is when the real you
takes a break from your personality.

Remove the first letter of loneliness
to find what is hidden within.

Some use drugs for the buzz of adrenaline,
others use anger, fear, trauma....

Who sees the game more clearly,
the spectator,
or the player desperate to win?

'Around the corner'
holds fear for the pessimist
and excitement for the optimist.

Children don't suffer with guilt
(and we're supposed to be the grown ups?)

Only what won't be given,
can be taken.

Arguments fear apologies.

When financial assets appreciate,
they go up in value.
The same happens with people.

Respect can free you to accept
what you can't understand.

Death is a very expensive experience,
in fact it will cost you everything.

When you live the future,
it becomes the now.

Through your perceptions
you can change **anything.**

The journey **is** the destination.

How many would you give
your self worth out of ten?

Because that's the amount of power you give
to the only piece of equipment
with which you can experience your life.

Memories, like computers,
don't always give us
what we want on the screen,
but it's all in there somewhere.

Optimists have all the luck!

The most difficult relationship
you will ever be in,
is the one with yourself.
It's the one you can't walk out of.

The arrow that misses the target
often travels further...

Remember...
you are pure love with skin on.

Don't waste ill health,
use it to heal your life.

Happiness and Sadness;
Two tears that look the same
but taste very different.

A scholar observing life
sees an unwelcome outcome as a lesson.
A victim sees it as just more bad luck!

Death is merely
a more advanced form of living.

<u>How to experience a million miracles a day:</u>

Step 1.
Consider the miracle of modern technology.

Step 2.
Focus on the fact
that the whole of modern technology
cannot reproduce a single blade of grass.

Step 3.
Find a lawn.

The optimist and the pessimist:
Each produce a crop
to satisfy their own appetite.

Stained glass windows,
like beliefs,
allow us many different ways
to see the one light.
Regardless, the brightest place
is the other side of the window.

Constant analysis
can cause paralysis.

Do you **enjoy** what might happen
as much as you **fear** what might happen?

When perseverance
meets a good idea,
it's only a matter of time...

Eyes which look to darkness
do not reflect the sun.

Using yourself
as a gauge for others
is guaranteed to wind you up
in a world where everyone is different.

The quality control of your life
is how you think.
Everything must pass through it.

Priorities are the creators of destinies.

Why deny others
the opportunity
of feeling good about themselves
by not asking a favour of them?

Other may press your buttons,
but it's up to you
what comes up on the screen.

Trust
is
letting go.

The only real victim of hatred
is its creator.

What we give out
is multiplied and returned.
So watch what you give out!

Blame is a prison
which holds many victims.

Growing pains of the soul
are often confused
with a breaking heart.

Some people think this is it;
fish think the same about the sea.

In your whole life,
your greatest test
will be to get on with those
with whom you don't agree.

Confidence and ability
are not related.

Trying to change people,
is the same as giving your optician
the things you would like
to see more clearly!

Emptiness
is simply
a lack of dreams.

Someone may put out the candle,
but that isn't the end of fire.

Infatuation is often mistaken for love,
until it's anesthetic wears off....ouch!

God can't get through
while your line is engaged.

Unconditional loving.
That includes **you!**

A 'permanent positive attitude',
would be like
trying to draw on white paper
with a white pen.
We need the contrast to create the picture.

Darkness is black,
light is all colours.

One stone was broken in two,
and cried,
'Now I am only half the stone I was'.
Another stone was broken in two,
and cried,
'Now I am twice the stone I was'.

Out of all the wonders
in all the world,
the most incredible thing,
in your whole life,
is already inside you.

Life reciprocates your beliefs of it.

Gossip only affects those who listen to it.

The past
is like a field of grass -
it looks greener from a distance.

Silence is amplified
after a lot of noise.

Just follow the signs for desire,
as you drive away
from a place called contentment.

'It can't get any worse'
- the climb that creates the fall.

Love and Hate:
The same flame that lights the candle
can burn the house down!

Troubled waters can be crossed
using a bridge called friendship.

'Learning more',
can be a clever way to avoid
applying what we already know.

Change can't be stopped,
but people try.
We call this trauma.

Sometimes people confuse
a new opening in their life with a hole,
and a great opportunity is missed.

The traveller needs to let go
of each step along his journey.

Just because they're your beliefs,
don't be fooled into thinking
that they always act in your best interests.

Progress and change.
They have about as much in common
as flame and fire.

Earning a living
isn't getting a life.

A successful way of creating losers
is a competitive society.

The tree with the least leaves
gives less resistance to the storm.

A competitor
is a potential ally!

Books don't mean a lot
unless you open them,
hearts are the same...

Kindness is love in motion.

We want to change in others
what we can't accept in ourselves.

Your self worth
isn't the creation of your past,
it's the creator of your future.

Death is simply life
without ripples and wrinkles.

Wonderment exists
in every child
inside every adult.

'No time in heaven'
means that those who go on ahead
are never without us.

Your tolerance is best measured
by whatever conflicts with your beliefs.

Once upon a time
a 'travelling case'
turned into
a 'just incase'
and never went anywhere!

Wealth isn't contentment.
You can't buy contentment.
Contentment has to be found.

Things never go wrong.
They just don't always happen
how we would like.

Every time you 'get it wrong',
you increase the odds to 'get it right'.

Criticisms are opinions
belonging to others,
so don't take what isn't yours.

A fear starts when you think it,
and stops when you don't.

Everyone is gifted,
it's just that some leave the wrapping on
longer than others.

Impatient people wind up
being wound up
by the clock they use on others.

Courage is the leaf
that doesn't wait for Autumn...

A young woman once went in search of
'the path to follow'.
Her whole life she searched in vain.
Until, one day it was time to return to heaven.
So she stopped her searching
and turned to bid her past farewell.
Never before had she looked behind
her gaze had always been ahead - searching for
'the path to follow'.
Instantly her heart was filled with a great joy.
There it was - at last!
'the path to follow'.
But then she realised what had happened
and her heart was filled with a great sadness.
For though she had found,
'the path to follow'
she could see that this path,
the path she had searched for all her life,
was in fact the path that she had made herself,
whilst searching for....
'the path to follow'

ACKNOWLEDGMENTS

In addition to those in volume one...

David Brough
I have little doubt that this man came to earth as an Angel

David Sargeant
whose search for wisdom is an inspiration to me

Iris Oakman
whose serenity still warms me from paradise, where she lives now

Martin & Lorraine
who didn't lend me their support - they gave it

Sharon Veal
living proof of the awesome power of friendship

If you feel this is meant for you -
it's because it is....

Please Believe these words

Please believe these words.
Before I couldn't always be with you,
but that's all changed now, you see, there's no time in heaven,
which means I can never be without you, so - I'm always with you.
I'm with you now, as you read these words.
I can see things much more clearly than before.
I see that the biggest part of us always remains in heaven,
and only a tiny consciousness comes to earth.
So you see, the bigger part of you is here with me now.
It's not so easy to see me like before, but that's OK,
it's only because you're looking through that tiny earth bound consciousness.
I was brought back because I was needed to be closer to God and to you.
Heaven is even better than I thought it would be,
you see, it isn't a place, it's a feeling.
Imagine the most wonderful feeling - ever,
times it by the biggest number - ever.
Well that's where I live now.
Heaven is far too wonderful to be a place, things can happen to places,
they're a bit like bodies, that's why we don't need them here.
It's OK if you doubt what I'm saying - it's just that there's no doubt in heaven.
If you're wondering why I talk as if you're not with me,
it's only because I'm talking to that tiny earth bound part of you,
and when that tiny part is ready to be released,
you'll know then what I know now.
Please don't hurry to be with me - you already are.
We have eternity, I can see it, it's so wonderful.
The rest of your life could seem long,
but remember, it's only a tiny consciousness in eternity.
Allow yourself to grieve - it's natural.
Allow yourself to doubt - it's natural.
Remember, I'm always with you - it's natural.
The pain you feel, I understand, but know your tears are not needed for me,
how can they be when I stand in heaven next to you?
All our good times are not gone, I'm in them still, and you're with me.
Listen - no stranger wrote these words - Our love did....
There are no good-byes, no farewells,
how can there be when you're with me now,
just as I am with you, always.
So I'll wait with you, until you like me are freed,
freed from that tiny, tiny consciousness called life.
Until then, I ask just one thing of you,
Please believe these words.......

RW